OF

RICA

The publisher wishes to thank proud Mainers
Julie Falatko, Rebekah Lowell, and Kalee Gwarjanski
for generously adding their local knowledge to this book.

Text copyright © 2021 by Penguin Random House LLC
Cover art and interior illustrations copyright © 2021 by Åsa Gilland

All rights reserved. Published in the United States by Doubleday, an imprint of
Random House Children's Books, a division of Penguin Random House LLC, New York.

Doubleday and the colophon are registered trademarks of Penguin Random House LLC.

Visit us on the Web! rhcbooks.com

Educators and librarians, for a variety of teaching tools, visit us at RHTeachersLibrarians.com

*Library of Congress Cataloging-in-Publication Data*
Names: Gilland, Åsa, author, illustrator.
Title: Welcome to Maine / by Åsa Gilland.
Description: First edition. | New York : Doubleday, [2021] | Audience: Ages 3–7
Summary: "An illustrated introduction to the state of Maine" —Provided by publisher.
Identifiers: LCCN 2020018226 (print) | LCCN 2020018227 (ebook) |
ISBN 978-0-593-30810-3 (trade) | ISBN 978-0-593-30811-0 (ebook)
Subjects: LCSH: Maine—Juvenile literature.
Classification: LCC F19.3 .G55 2021 (print) | LCC F19.3 (ebook) | DDC 974.1—dc23

MANUFACTURED IN CHINA
10 9 8 7 6 5 4 3 2 1
First Edition

# WELCOME to MAINE

illustrated by Åsa Gilland

Doubleday Books for Young Readers

# WELCOME to MAINE!

## WE'RE GLAD YOU'RE HERE!

ALASKA

WASHINGTON

OREGON

MONTANA

NORTH DAKOTA

MINNESOTA

WISCONSIN

MICHIGAN

IDAHO

WYOMING

SOUTH DAKOTA

NEW YO

CALIFORNIA

NEVADA

UTAH

COLORADO

NEBRASKA

IOWA

ILLINOIS

INDIANA

OHIO

PENNSYLVANIA

WEST VIRGINIA

KANSAS

MISSOURI

KENTUCKY

VIRGINIA

ARIZONA

NEW MEXICO

OKLAHOMA

ARKANSAS

TENNESSEE

NORTH CAROLINA

SOUTH CAROLINA

TEXAS

LOUISIANA

MISSISSIPPI

ALABAMA

GEORGIA

FLORIDA

Hawaii

MAINE

AUGUSTA

NEW HAMPSHIRE
MASSACHUSETTS
RHODE ISLAND
CONNECTICUT

W JERSEY
WARE
LAND

DIRIGO

MAINE

Capital city: Augusta
State nickname: The Pine Tree State
State motto: "Dirigo" ("I Lead")

MOOSEHEAD LAKE

MILLINOCKET

BANGOR

AUGUSTA

LEWISTON

AUBURN

PORTLAND

FREEPORT

BAR HARBOR

KENNEBUNKPORT

KITTERY

# MAINE

**FORT KENT**

**PRESQUE ISLE**

**CALAIS**

**GULF OF MAINE**

If you love to play outdoors, Maine is the state for you! You can hike through pine forests, climb mountains, dig for clams at the seashore, and go boating in the Atlantic Ocean.

Maine's state animal is the moose, and there are lots of them here. It's always exciting to see one, so keep your eyes open! The males have huge antlers, which they shed and regrow once a year.

If you fill a bird feeder with sunflower seeds, you might meet Maine's state bird, the chickadee. Chickadees have a little cap of colored feathers on their head.

Maine is covered in forests, and the state tree is the Eastern white pine. This kind of tree doesn't have flat leaves. Instead, it has needles, which stay green year-round.

PORTLAND HEAD LIGHT

What's that tall, skinny building near the ocean? It's a lighthouse, and Maine has over sixty of them. Their bright lights keep boats from crashing into the shore. Maine's oldest and most famous one is the Portland Head Light.

Have you read a book called *Goodnight Moon*? It was written by Margaret Wise Brown, who once lived on Vinalhaven. She also wrote *The Little Island*, about a tiny island in Penobscot Bay.

MARGARET WISE BROWN

And have you read *Charlotte's Web, Blueberries for Sal,* or *Miss Rumphius*? They were written by Maine authors, too: E. B. White, Robert McCloskey, and Barbara Cooney.

Maine's tallest mountain is Katahdin, in Baxter State Park. It's at the northern end of the Appalachian Trail, which you could follow south through fourteen states to Springer Mountain, in Georgia.

The Penobscot Native Americans gave Katahdin its name, which means "the Greatest Mountain."

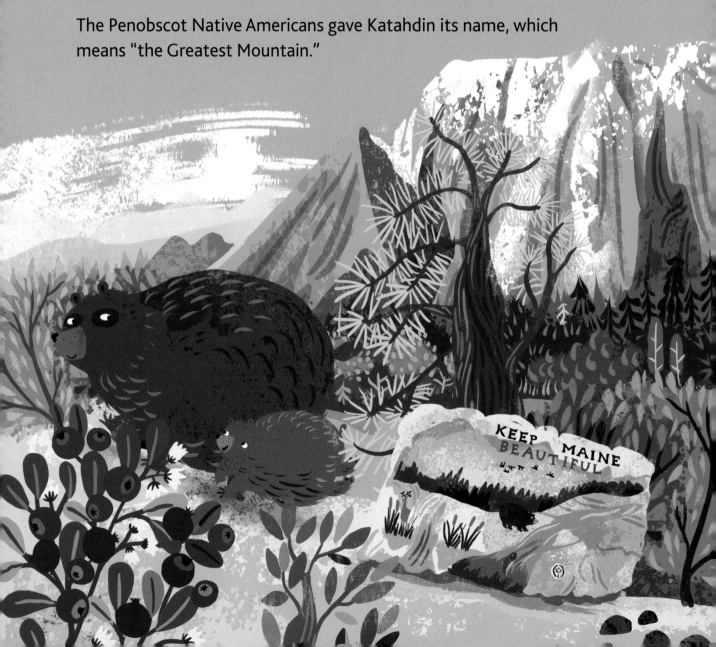

KEEP MAINE BEAUTIFUL

# ACADIA
## NATIONAL PARK

People come from around the world to visit beautiful Acadia National Park. You can camp under the stars, go canoeing or kayaking, and hike up Cadillac Mountain, where you can see for miles.

CADILLAC
SOUTH RIDGE TRAIL

CADILLAC
WEST FACE TRAIL

CADILLAC MTN. 5MI .8KM

3.7MI BLACKWOODS
6.0KM CAMPGROUND

You're going to be hungry after all that outdoor fun!
Luckily, there's a lot to eat in Maine.

POTATOES

MAPLE SYRUP

MAINE MAPLE SYRUP

APPLES

BLUEBERRY PIE

CHOWDER

WHOOPIE PIE

LOBSTER

RED SNAPPER HOT DOG

FIDDLEHEADS

BAKED BEANS

ITALIAN SANDWICH

FRIED CLAMS

CANNED BROWN BREAD

WHICH one is your FAVORITE?

A great state like Maine has a lot of unusual things to see if you're out for a drive:

# DESERT ᴏꜰ MAINE

You'll find deserts in hot states like Arizona and Nevada. But in the green state of Maine? This sandy area in Freeport looks like a desert, so it got the nickname Desert of Maine. There's also a sand museum, with sand sent by people from all over the world.

# PAUL BUNYAN STATUE

Did you ever hear the story of Paul Bunyan, the giant lumberjack? Some say he was born in Bangor. If you visit, you can see a giant statue of this famous woodsman, thirty-one feet high. Now, that's a tall tale!

# LENNY THE CHOCOLATE MOOSE

You'll find the sweetest moose in Maine at the Len Libby candy shop, in Scarborough. Lenny is a life-size moose made of chocolate!

If you love Maine, then you're a Maine kid!
And Maine kids are the best!